The Horse Knows the Way

The Horse Knows the Way

Poems by

Dave Margoshes

BuschekBooks
Ottawa

Library and Archives Canada Cataloguing in Publication

Margoshes, Dave\
    The horse knows the way : poems / by Dave Margoshes.

Poems.
ISBN 978-1-894543-57-6

    I. Title.

PS8576.A647H67 2009   C811'.54   C2009-904252-5

Cover image: Black Horse in a Winter Field, iStockphoto image #7295508, used with permission.

Printed in Canada by Hignell Book Printing, Winnipeg, Manitoba.

BuschekBooks acknowledges the support of the Canada Council for the Arts which last year invested $20.1 million in writing and publishing throughout Canada.

**Canada Council
for the Arts**

**Conseil des Arts
du Canada**

Acknowledgments:

Both this collection and the title poem, "The Horse Knows the Way," owe a tip of the hat to two sources: the obvious one, Robert Frost's amazing poem "Stopping by Woods on a Snowy Evening," from which a few images are borrowed; the other, John O'Hara's 1964 story collection of the same title. A few of these poems have appeared in the following literary magazines: *Antigonish Review, Canadian Literature, Existere, in media res, Kaleidoscope, MTLS* (online), and *Queen's Quarterly*; and the anthology *Arms Like Ladders: the Eloquent She* (published by the League of Canadian Poets Feminist Caucus). "Floating in Land" was commissioned by the Regina dance troupe New Dance Horizons and appears on its website, www. newdancehorizons.ca. "Becoming a writer" was included in *The Best Canadian Poetry, 2009* (Tightrope Books). My thanks to the editors involved, and to Donna Caruso, whose *Life Without Borders* television show on SCN in Saskatchewan featured several of these poems in video form. My thanks too to Bob Currie and John Buschek for their sharp eyes and support.

The line quoted from Louise Halfe's book *Blue Marrow* in "The moving finger" is copyrighted by Louise B. Halfe and is used with permission and thanks.

The lines quoted from Wendy McNeil's song "She prayed" in "A Promise" are copyrighted by Wendy McNeil and are used with permission and thanks.

The line by Eugene McNamara alluded to in "A boy in Danville" is from the poem "Square Dancing in Naperville," copyrighted by Eugene McNamara and is used with permission and thanks.

The line "It's only a matter of time until we shine" quoted in "Until we shine" is from the Junkhouse song "Shine," by Tom Wilson and Colin Cripps and is copyrighted by Tom Wilson; used with permission and thanks.

for my sisters, Esther and Judy

Table of Contents

Acknowledgements...3

An imagined life
    A tinfoil mobile   11
    The chicken coop   12
    Living above the bagel factory   13
    An American dream, 1952   14
    Sisters from space   15
    Brooklyn summer   16
    Becoming a writer   17
    Catalpa   18
    The hunter   19
    Neshanic Mountain   20
    Starry, starry night   21
    A face in a window   22
    More than a dream   23
    Turn the page   24
    Back in Banff   26
    A girl of my dreams   27
    Waking before light   28
    My inner child   29
    An itch   30
    Delancy Street   31
    News from home   32
    Autobiography   33
    Something about a wall   34
    Ellis Island   35
Six degrees of separation
    The letter carrier pauses to refresh her lipstick   41
    The horse knows the way   42
    Lost and found   43
    About Icarus   44
    The moving finger   45
    Prologue to the slaver's journal   46
    Hands   47

The poem the fox wrote   48
Thirteen ways of looking at a black woman   49
Brooklyn girls   50
The swimmers   51
Bait   52
Addressee unknown   53
Moscow was burning   54
The contender   55
The singing   56
Screenplay by King   58
Homecoming   59
Six degree of separation   60
Smoking   62
Oedipus   64
Doing better   65
West by west   66
At Frost's grave, Bennington, Vermont   67
The elements
Rough weather   71
Lucky old sun   72
Seventy is nothing   73
Extremes   74
The four elements   75
Bad luck dog   76
Saskatchewan weather report   77
Hollow bones   78
Hands, mouth, teeth   79
Making dirt   80
Mushrooms   81
Floating in land   82
Sister moon   83
Being   84
Black ice   85
White on white   86
The tick   87
Aurora borealis   88
Tea and sympathy   89
The hunger   90

The vanity of trees   91
The hour   92
Morning in the Retreat House   93
Where the heart goes
    The romance of sport   97
    Shoulda, woulda, coulda   98
    Where the heart goes   99
    A winter of discontent   100
    The way love is   101
    Lilacs don't bloom here   102
    Head over heels   103
    Heart's warning   104
    Eyes full of birds   105
    Beautiful   106
    Music of water   107
    What I miss   108
    Vanity   109
    A promise   110
    Land mines   111
    Home and garden   112
    To the station   113
    Wreckless moon   114
    Scars   115
    A boy in Danville   116
    Taking chances   117
    Spring in the seasons of trees   118
    What moves   119
    Until we shine   120

An imagined life

A tinfoil mobile

I remember so well the first time
my parents made love after my birth.
I lay in the bassinette gazing open-mouthed
at the tinfoil mobile my father had constructed
and hung above me, while in the bed
across the room my father and mother
came together with a hunger
I could appreciate, my father seeking
a return to the shaded world from which I
had so latterly emerged. It had been warm there,
I remembered, and snug, but banal and dull,
and I wondered why he sought with such urgency
to go there when I was *here*. I heard my mother
cry out, as I knew I so often did, and later, while
she fitfully slept, I heard her murmur. She dreamt
first of my father, then of me, and I watched
expressions sweep across her face as she foresaw
the pleasures and pain we would bring her.
Above me the mobile danced in time
with the rhythms of this spinning globe
upon which we lived, just a concoction
of the linings from packets of cigarettes twisted
in various shapes and fishing line, almost transparent.
How strange, I thought, these blind urges of men
and women, and like my mother I slept and dreamt,
dreamt of the man I would some day be.

The chicken coop

The house my parents had built
for them went back to the bank
and we moved three miles down
the road to a chicken coop converted
to a crude home, and that's where I
learned first to crawl, then
to walk. Later, we moved deep
into an orchard of apples and pears
to an abandoned farmhouse
with a pond and snapping turtles
and eels. No chickens but geese
chasing the dogs with their eel necks
curved and it's here that I learned
to run, to talk, that I became the first part
of what I am. My father never overcame
his sadness at the loss of the house
he'd first drawn on a napkin at the Automat
on Lower Broadway—the house was gone
but he still had that napkin, crumpled
in the dresser drawer where he kept
folded money and his glasses. "It doesn't matter
how many new floors, how many coats
of paint," he would complain in his glass
of port, "you never get rid of the stink
of chickens." And he'd point
an uncertain finger at me. "Don't you
forget that. It's who you are."

Living above the bagel factory

Four in the morning the bakers below would start
and by 5 the air in my dreams was rich with yeast
and onion, leavening them, sharpening them. My mouth
watered me awake and my mother would send me
stumbling in my underpants into the hallway and down
two flights, where the white-handed baker would wink
and hand me a bag of half a dozen assorted, poppy
and egg, still hot from the oven, so chewy there was
no need for butter or jam. They were free, the royalty
paid us for allowing our dreams to be sweetened.
When we moved away it was the bagels my sisters
and I missed most. They married and I was left
alone, tossing on my scentless bed. Would I ever
sleep that well again?

An American dream, 1952

Ike came to New York. Was he there
as President or as candidate? I don't know.
I was a boy and not aware of the details
or nuances of politics. There was a caravan,
a long line of shiny black cars, moving
slowly down Eastern Parkway, where we
lived. The crowd lining the sidewalk was
thick as any you'd see at Coney Island
or Ebbets Field and I was small, alone.
But people parted the way the Bible says
the Red Sea did for Moses, and I was
in the front, and then a car was stopping,
a man was waving from the window. I was
pushed forward by a fat woman who smelled
of lilacs and Ike was saying, "What's *your* name,
young man?" "Davey," I said. "A fine name,"
Ike said, and he shook my hand as if I were a man
and we were the best of friends, and the limousine
moved forward. "Bet you won't wash that hand
for a week," a grinning man said and that's what
I would have done but Momma said, "Wash up
for dinner, Davey," and I forgot.

Sisters from space
        (for Es & J)

When I was a boy my older sisters
were Martians, tall graceful creatures
from a distant planet who had learned
our language, learned to pass, fooling
even my father and mother but not me.
They were not hostile, these aliens,
one with her long blonde braid, the other
with her books and laughter, but not
entirely benign; they had no need
for force for they could kill with a look,
a word chosen carefully—no, *carelessly*—
could maim. I learned the signs, knew when
to take cover, how to defend myself, but still
they left scars. Eventually, as I grew older
they grew into themselves, allowed themselves
to forget that other world they'd come from.
The radioactivity that used to pulse beneath
their perfumed skin cooled, but their power
over me continued, continues even now
as we grow old. They may have forgotten
who they are but I haven't. In the dark, when
they thought I was sleeping, my eyes
were open, I saw them.

Brooklyn summer

Candy store on the corner,
stacks of newspaper on the stand,
the boys leaning on parked-car fins,
a smell of chocolate syrup and fizzy water,
tobacco smoke. The moon so close
you can almost touch it—*watch it,*
watch it, it's hot, sharp. No, nothing
sharp, just the sulky evening
spreading itself out against the street
like the scent trailing that girl,
the click of heels passing.

Becoming a writer

What could be easier than learning to write?
Novels, poems, fables with and without morals,
they're all within you, in the heart, the head,
the bowel, the tip of the pen a diviner's rod.
Reach inside and there they are, the people
one knows, their scandalous comments,
the silly things they do, the unforgettable feeling
of a wet eyelash on your burning cheek.
This moment, that, an eruption of violence,
a glancing away, the grandest of entrances,
the telling gesture, the banal and the beautiful,
all conspire with feeling and passion to transport,
to deliver, to inspire. Story emerges
from this cocoon, a crystalline moment, epiphanies
flashing like lightbulbs above the heads
of cartoon characters. All this within you
where you least expect it, not so much in the head
as under the arms, glistening with sweat, stinking
with the knowledge of the body, the writer
neither practitioner nor artisan but miner, digging
within himself for riches unimagined, for salt.

Catalpa

I lay beneath the fragrant catalpa tree
smoking a crude cigarette
of hawthorn leaf and catalpa silk
and let myself flow into the dizziness
it brought rather than resist it, let it lift me
as if I were a feather or one of the clouds
drifting above, that one in the shape
of a dog, that one that looks like a bull.
Catalpa, alpaca, Cadillac, catamaran. I grew
drowsy with the possibilities, tipsy
with the feelings that rippled
through me on the summer breeze.
Was I drunk? Intoxicated, yes,
as only a child in love with the future
can be. My eyes were closed
but I could see perfectly, I could see
everything.

The hunter

We lived when I was a boy not in the woods
but near enough that I could walk in them
at my will, and Saturdays I would take
the dogs and go, the dogs leading the way
like a flashlight's beam braving the first edge
of darkness, Robbie and Lady wild
with the madness of ticks and the illusion
of freedom played by the wind. In autumn
when I was 14 and 15 and 16 I liked to carry
my shotgun crooked in the bend of my arm
as if it were at the ready, though it was empty
and the shells in my pocket were not likely
to be fitted into the oiled dark throat
of the gun's hunger. There was no more chance
of my killing a grouse than there was of Robbie
turning his teeth on me, so little harm
in either of us. That wasn't always true. We
had both killed birds, the dog in the blindness
of his being, me in some faint hope that it
would transform me into a man, 13, the sudden
eruption of force against my shoulder
and its lingering ache, the long, sad fall
of the crumpled wing into the bushes,
the hysteria of the dogs, their tongues bursting
from their long mouths, and my own silence,
the bitter smell of gunpowder sharp in my nostrils,
the small death in my open hand, the surprise
of my diminishment, more a child then
than ever.

Neshanic Mountain

My father drove the truck, me in the back
with the dogs, up the winding road
to Neshanic Mountain where the hillbillies
lived, past their hardscrabble camps to where
the creek had run dry and stones lay like
fallen apples from God's own tree ripe
for the picking. "Watch out for snakes,"
my father said, putting on his gloves,
but I had trust the dogs would scare them
away. All day we picked the best we could,
flat splinters of soft shale we wrestled
from the creek bed and long islands
of broken granite, filling the back
of the truck. For weeks later at home
my father followed a blueprint in his mind
to arrange them, just so, into a wall
God never had in his design. In the end, only
snakes thanked him, finding a home away
from home in the wall's shade, doing
God's slow work in bringing down what
He hadn't wanted.

Starry, starry night

The stars so bright, the night so dark.
I had forgotten darkness could be
so complete, stars so loud, shouting
to make themselves heard over each other.
Where I live, in the city, the stars are strangers,
struggling to say their small piece. Here they
are vain, boasting their purity of light.

There is a rope around the tree
outside my cabin, as if someone feared
it might run off, but where would it go? All
it needs, all it could be, is here, its feet
shod in earth, its head lost in stars, leaves
dreaming. I would take that cue if I could,
stand here motionless for years, rooted
to a place I cannot understand, my eyes
weeping stars. I wouldn't need a rope
to hold me here, no rope could pull me
away, not this dark night. Look down
and stumble. Look up, everything is clear.

A face in a window

Once, in a used bookstore in Calgary,
from behind a shelf I looked up and through
the front window and saw your face framed
in the window of a bus that had paused
at the corner. You were looking straight
ahead and I didn't think you would but
in a moment you turned and your gaze
travelled through two panes of glass
to me, too far away to see the colour
of your eyes but close enough to see
your intent. Did I imagine the flicker
of a smile, or was it a distortion
in the glass, waves of August heat, fumes
rising giddily from the bus? That was years
ago and you and I both live far away
from that place now. We don't see each other,
don't stay in touch. Still, the heat
of your gaze is on me, it reddens my face.
The bus quivers like a race horse but across
the arm's length of distance and time
I imagine the quiver is mine.

More than a dream

I woke from a dream that was more
than a dream, and less. I was a boy
I'd never been in a world
disarmingly familiar, holding
clammy hands with a girl I thought
I might have known somewhere else.
We were in line outside the classroom,
the bitter smell of oilcloth and galoshes
and Irish stew in our nostrils. The rope
of dirty blond hair at the back of her head
was unruly and damp, like a sleek dark animal
I had seen in a creek, but that was
in another dream, a dream easier to accept
for what it was. This dream baffled me
with its cunning, its cynicism. Why
would a dream turn on you that way,
holding its breath, sticking out its tongue?
I woke and shook my head, refusing
to believe its promise. All day I thought
first of the girl, the gap between her teeth,
the slow ticking of the clock on the wall
above her radiant head, then of the creek
in the dream I longed to return to,
longed to plunge into, to drown.

Turn the page

A woman whose demons are howling too loudly
takes her baby and sacrifices herself
on the altar of the subway, looking for peace.
Halfway across the country, another woman,
another set of demons, a curiously small child
in a grocery cart, a note. And halfway across
the world, a submarine, the bottom of the sea, time
spinning itself out.

I'm a news junky but it doesn't take me long
to read the paper, breakfast and a second cup
of coffee. Years of practice make short work
of crime and politics, too much of this, not enough
of that, I can usually predict the end of a quote,
the way a story will turn. These stories are
different, holding my attention through the week
as they run their sad course, one mother finally dying
after holding onto the thread for days, another mother
found, her story spilling out surprisingly banal,
the rescuers finally making it to the hatch but too late,
the seas rough, always the seas rough, the same
rough seas we all navigate. A third cup of coffee
as I speculate on the probability of three such stories
occurring at the same time, enough to give a news junky
an overdose. Those faces gazing out of the newspaper
with such equanimity, happier days, a submariner
on his wedding day, the haunted mother in her cap
and gown, the peculiar child grinning, a toy truck
in his chubby hand.

Their lives demand attention, they call out
to the reader anxious to get to the sports page,
the comics, the horoscope, transfixing us, *put aside*
the complexities of global warming, global economies,
our stories are so simple, send us a poet to record them
not a reporter. Send us Chekhov. But the men are
drowned, one mother dead, the other found, the faces
and stories recede. The sports page calls, or doesn't.
Another cup of coffee.
Turn the page.

Back in Banff

First day back in Banff
after a dozen years or more
my eyes fill with the familiar
and the changed, the curious gaze
of an elk cow, garbage cans
shining with attitude, the resigned shrug
on the shoulders of shopgirls, the punctilious trails
behind the hotel already seducing the aching pop
from my knees, almost as if I were still 30
and my feet light as breath, the breath
taken from me now. The sisters
raise their white-nostriled noses as they
always have, the tinfoil townsite crackling
beneath the weight of cameras and desire,
the delirious stink of sulfur egging its way
under my skin. Deep in, high up, off
the beaten path in her lair, the grizzly sniffs the air
as she rolls over in her sleep, dreaming
of our meeting on the trail. She trembles.

A girl of my dreams

A dark-haired beauty flits through my dreams like a deer
glimpsed in a woods, a motion here, a blur, a flash of colour,
for one heart-stopping moment a vivid revelation, the deer
materializing in a space between leaves to glance with a mixture
of alarm and curiosity at me, all velvet and surprise. But the
woman in my dream will not face me. It is the back of her head
I see in the distance, a blurred profile, a whirl of sable hair. I
see the shape of her hips through her cloak, the breadth of her
shoulders, one slim arm curved like a scythe. In wet grass, the
impression of one small foot.

Waking, it is the fan of her hair that catches in my throat, that
lingers with me as I rise and shower and dress, only gradually to
fade over breakfast. It doesn't matter. I know that she will come
again, tonight and tomorrow night. She has been the compan-
ion of my bed for as long as I can remember now, always wilful,
always reluctant.

I have read Freud and I know the signs. She is a secret lover,
that goes without saying. She is my mother, my sister, an
unrequited sweetheart of childhood. She is death, birth, a
new beginning, a bad end. A wet spot, a dry spell. A swallow
of blood. She brushes her hair with a silver-backed brush, one
hundred strokes.

Then she shakes her head.

Waking before light

Waking before light, you don't know
if it's the middle of the night
or just before dawn, whether you're
still locked in the life you lived
yesterday or have slipped into the freedom
of today, where anything is possible. You
stand by the window watching and listening
for clues, the rumble of traffic
at the corner or the heartbreaking flash
of the milkman's door opening
onto the cold. The warmth of the bed
calls out to you but in that comfort
is the decay of all you've left behind,
the persistent finger in the rib, and
but for this halfway moment
with its cruel uncertainty
you know today can be different.

My inner child

The child within me is too close. Today
I seek to touch something older, further
away, the serpent in me, the fish. I long
to recline in the sun, indifferent to the affairs
of others, to float bristling in a sea plangent
with opportunity to eat and be eaten. I would like
to shed my skin, coil naked-nerved beside it
and admire its fragile translucent beauty,
would love to rub my scales against coral
and gulp at the elusive insinuation of oxygen
processed through my gills, secure and smug
in my glistening soapless bath, feel the thrill
of the primitive, that time before the child
within me began to cry.

An itch

The itch begins between my toes
and rises quickly to my ankles, shins,
thighs, private places. Soon I'm shuddering
in the shower as the steam brings relief
to my shoulders and ribs, then luxuriating
in the cat's tongue of a rough towel. But
in my clothes there's no relief, no way
of reaching the spot between
the blades. My scalp tingles, the tips
of my fingers raw with the exertion
of scratching where I can. A bee's buzz
rises from my body, a hummingbird's
tremble. All day I am not in agony,
but anticipation, how long can this
last, I wonder, where else can it go?
At last I lie writhing in bed, the sheets
more a torment than solace, not cool
but coy, smug, they know so much
about me, so much yet so little
they're willing to tell.

Delancy Street

Crossing Delancy, I came upon a child selling
flowers, three for a nickel. They were daisies,
yellow and bright-faced but roughly cut
with a dull knife from the bully garden
of the fishmonger's wife around the corner,
I'd wager, and God only knows what she
will think when she comes home. I stopped
to buy half a dozen and pinned the nicest one
to my lapel. "That's a whole dime,"
the girl exclaimed and I gladly gave it to her,
though I had but two dimes in my pocket,
knowing full well she'd put it to better use
than I ever would. I spent my other dime
on a plate of clams and oh, they tasted good
beside the pint of cold beer they came with,
and my, the daisies looked fine in that pint
jar afterwards. Let them laugh at that bar, I
don't care, I have those daisies, the clams
and the beer in my belly, and that precious child
has a dime to feed *her* family. It's a new world,
and all I've been told about it has been right.

News from home

My sister calls with the news, good and bad. Sally's cancer incurable, but some people are known to live long lives with it. Uncle Bob's mental disorder, kept secret all these years, out in the open now, now that Aunt Flo has Alzheimer's, but they're both comfortable in the care home. This niece still out of work, but in love; that one jilted but doing well. Even my sister's stocks have gone south, the wealth they enjoyed on paper for a while gone but, she says, "at least we bought the car."

For every cloud there is the expected silver lining, for every flash of silver, a cloud. Those so inclined may keep score but I put my faith in this balancing out, thick and thin, sickness and health, richer poorer. There will come a day when my sister and I say goodbye a last time, she a few years older but I living more dangerously, it's hard to say which way the odds will fall. Grieving is a luxury only the living can afford, the dead wrapping themselves in flashes of silver.

Autobiography

I burned my bridges, lit the fire myself.
I trimmed my wings and sang the old
sad song they sing as they march home
from war, their armour lost, swords beaten
into plowshares. I kept my own counsel,
hoisted myself on my own petard, I watched
my tongue, bit my lip. Whatever advice
there was I both flouted and followed,
doing myself whatever harm I could.
When the time came to stand with hand
out I curled mine into a fist. I rolled
with the punches, I pulled no punches,
shed no tears. I drank too much, sang
too loudly; I looked too long at the sun
and went blind. I burned my bridges,
one by one. I called out, but I had no voice.

Something about a wall
              (In memory of Sarah Shalley Goldberg)

The night after my aunt died
my father slipped into my dreams
to scold me for having let the stones
in the wall we worked so hard to build
fall apart, the mortar of mud and grass
we'd used to chink the cracking shale
nosed aside by garter snakes seeking
the comfort of sun. But that was all
long ago, I protested, and thousands
of miles from where I now lived. My father
frowned his disapproval and turned back
to the work, his hands thick with pebbles
and sand, a paste of milkweed juice
and spit, hands his own death had failed
to smooth. In the dream, there was
a wheelbarrow like the red one
we'd used, like the red one that mattered
so much, although that was something else
entirely, and my father had loaded it up
with tools and the material we'd need
to set matters right again. Something
about a wall nature takes offense to, though,
but he only laughed when I reminded him.
Something about a wall that calls out
for mending, he told me, something
that holds us all together.

Ellis Island
(after Jan Zwicky's "Robinson's Crossing"
and Robert Kroetsch's "The New World and Finding It")

1.

My father said they walked for seven days sustained by a lunch
of sausage, black bread, raw potatoes and cold tea in a can,
a feast in the first days, then a meal barely fit to eat. It was
summer and they found wormy apples beside the road, so deli-
cious, slept beneath their fragrance. On hill's brow overlooking
Odessa harbour, his mother, my *buba*, fell on her knees and
wept, but my father said, "Don't cry, Mama, it is only wheat,"
a deep, long field of blue wheat rolling in the wind, that's how
the sea seemed to him, his boyish eyes. The Black Sea, blue.

2.

Ellis Island. It's not like Long Island, a place where people live.
Not like Coney Island, where you go for the day, to have a good
time. More like Devil's Island, for some, right from the ship
into quarantine and back again, good riddance.

It's a museum now. My cousin Susanna sends me an email with
the website. She has found our mothers' names on the mani-
fest of a ship sailing from Southampton, 1912. A woman, our
grandmother, and two children, Berte, 5, and Mars, 4. When I
see this on the screen, something stops in my heart.

3.

I grew up only a few miles from it but I've never been there. I
never heard my mother mention it and, as for my father, just
this tale: "When we came off the boat, they took us aside and
gave us showers, made us wash our hair, looking for lice. All the
louses they let in," my father said, "but not any on us."

But I have come to understand just lately that it is my home, as
much my home as anywhere else I've been or haven't been, this
immigrant's life. My friends here in Saskatchewan speak of "the
family farm," "the homestead," the place their grandparents
came to, their first new home. I have come to think of Ellis
Island that way, a homestead, a home instead, a place that will
hold me in good stead, should I choose ever to go there.

4.

It is the place we all come from, the place we go, the place
where we pause in the moment as we live from moment to
moment, the place where the road divides. Ellis Island is the
purr of rain on grass, the rumble of rain's knuckles on the tin
roof, it is the thrum of cicadas singing the ancient song, the
pulse of blood in the well at the base of your lover's throat, the
beginning of things and the end, the unexpected metaphor, the
period at the end of the sentence. Ellis Island is the place we
never reach, never can reach, the point just beyond knowing.
It is what we see if we look too long upon the sun, the panoply
of stars behind the lids of our eyes, the last sound we hear after
we've turned out the light.

5.

Ellis Island. It is not a cry.
Not a map, not a blueprint.
It is a footprint. Just one.
In wet sand.
Facing west.

Six degrees of separation

The letter carrier pauses to refresh her lipstick

Mid-morning, mid-rounds, she takes
a half-block detour to her car, parked
in shade, handbag under the seat, compact,
mirror and a silvery tube of carmine gloss.
I am waiting for a bus, invisible, watching.
Mid-thirties, still nice-looking, dark hair
scissored short, body already making
the bewildering transformation from lean
to plush. Her lips purse, part, as if she
were kissing the air, or a transparent lover,
her hand rising to her face, pinkie tip
to the corner of her lips, eyebrow, smoothing,
smoothing. Perhaps a real lover awaits
in the next apartment block, rubbing
sleep from his eyes even now
in anticipation, or an early lunch calls her,
a proper restaurant meal with her husband.
Or perhaps I am not as invisible as I think.
I imagine I see her smile in the mirror.

The horse knows the way

The horse knows the way home
and I, by the grace of God, know
how to follow. Beneath us
and before us the road rolls out
like a black carpet of blood, the blood
pounding in our temples, whispering
its own secrets. Behind us a reflection
from the city of light shines,
shines. There is fear ahead
of us, behind us, below and above
but sense only in the way ahead, sense
and hope, that last refuge. The horse,
like Frost's, shakes his head, but
it is a dispassionate shake, a quiver
of faith. He may question
my impulses, but never his own. No,
the horse, thank God, knows the way,
and I, I know how to follow.

Lost and found

She was found at last in a snowdrift.
It was three days, and the men who came
upon her could only assume the worst. But
as they explained it later, a soft hollow
had been carved in the stiffened snow, as if
by a warm breath from God, and within it
the child slept as she might in her own bed,
her own breath regular, sure. When they awoke
her she cried out and what a blessed sound
that was. What could it be but a miracle, they
asked, yet why would God act this way, letting
her be lost only so she could be found? But is
that not the question the hymns ask us,
the scripture, the sermon? Think of Jonah cast
into the belly of the whale, Job and his boils, all
the lessons of Sunday School. Later, one
of the men returned to the spot, retracing
his singular footprints in the new-fallen snow,
counting each step, and thinking just such
thoughts. At the spot where they'd found
the child the careless wind had swept all trace
away and he stood as if in a dream, a dream
of a world in which the lost are found, the found
are lost, where pain is pleasure and pleasure
pain. He awoke from the dream to find
himself lost, with no hope of being found.

About Icarus
(after Williams and Brueghel*)

What we have perhaps failed to understand
about Icarus
is that he was not flying
but diving,
that in the water the wings his father so carefully fashioned
turned to fins,
that he swam and swam and swam
and lived with the fishes
forever.

*Based on William Carlos Williams' "Landscape with the fall
of Icarus," and the painting of the same title by Brueghel

The moving finger

A feather dipped in ink,*
snowshoe tracks on the snow-white
page, tracks the iconography
of birds, indecipherable to all
but magpies, those elementary
detectives, hungry clues. A serpent
dipped in ink, circumnavigating
the page like a tidal wave of tongues
whispering secrets we cannot know,
cannot tell, cannot keep. A hand
dipped in ink caressing my cheek,
staining its tattoo of love into my
teeth, teeth that fall out with rot, leaves
turning dry with brown neglect. A heart
dipped in ink, beating blue.

*from a line by Louise Halfe in *Blue Marrow*

Prologue to the slaver's journal

It was 1715 when I was impressed
into the slaver's life. I had gone to sea
the year before, a lad of 14, and knew not
what lay ahead. My first ship went aground
off the ivory coast and we were adrift
for but three days before a slaver headed in
took us aboard, all but our skipper, who'd gone
down, as he should, and the mate, who the men
had tossed out of the dory, no love lost there.
On shore, I was at loose ends but was given
shelter by a man of the cloth who took
an unusual liking to me and I was at my wit's end
when the mate of the slaver came round
to say there was a berth for me after all, should
I be on board that very afternoon. And so we
were back at sea with our ungodly cargo
before I really knew what I was about. I say
ungodly because if ever God looked away
it was when those wretched people were cast
into chains. They say His Eye is on the sparrow—
a flock of them must have had His attention
that sorry day. But they say too that He works
His wonders in mysterious ways, and my mother
in Heaven would smile if she knew the way
my own life has turned out, my share of bad,
oh yes, I won't deny that, much to be ashamed
of, but then there has been some good, the good
all the better for the bad, and more than one slave
will attest to that. It is of the good that, now
at the end of my long life, I intend to write.

Hands

God has no hands but ours
to carry on His work on Earth

In olden times, when paper
was scarce, people often wrote
on their hands, musical notations,
numbers, the name of a beloved-to-be.

The warrior, disarmed, extended
his hand in friendship. His enemy
was not deceived; he gave him the back
of his own hand.

In Sicily, to protect themselves, the poor
put their trust in a society of men
who placed their own faith in the strength
of the hand, the crude impression
of fingers and palms emblazoned in black.

Now I offer you my hand, take yours.
In the pocket my folded fingers form,
your hand is like the frightened heart
of an injured bird, beating, beating.

The poem the fox wrote

Today I caught my first sight of one
close up. I'd seen flashes before, through
leaves, always in motion, a blur of colour,
or from a distance as they came out
of their big den, preening in the sun,
but never so close, so long as today. I was
sitting on the shore contemplating
my philosophy as I do, and one came by,
in a slim shiny object floating on the water,
and oh what a grand sight. A magnificent coat,
all colours, the head dark in the back and ruffled,
pink and flattened in the front, so comical. She
looked right at me but didn't see. She drifted,
her head in the clouds as if she had not a care
or enemy in the world, and I watched her
for a long time. She arched her back, yawned,
scratched with a stick on a white square
in her lap. Thrilling! Later she came back
with more of them, her whole family, one
so big. They stood whispering on the shore
looking at something beyond me and I was able
to get closer still, could see their mouths opening
and closing, the shine of their teeth. When I moved
away finally, they followed, so bold, and I feared
they might be ill, too long in the sun. I went happy
to my den, curled into myself and dreamed of them.

Thirteen ways of looking at a black woman
(for Genie, Emily & Su-lin)

1. Head on.

2. At a slant.

3. From behind the lace arms of thorn trees in blossom.

4. With reverence, with respect, with admiration—and something else.

5. As if you were a soldier returning from a long campaign in Jerusalem, your hands stained, your face and heart scarred. You long for her touch, but you understand her apprehension.

6. As the shadowy men of Haddon would, with a certain reserve.

7. Through the tangled web of her hair, each strand twisted into a perfect pair, begging a question.

8. With a prayer. With resolve. With abandon.

9. Through a prism, the better to see the panoply of colour.

10. With caution. With courage.

11. From the umbrella of acacias, looking down; from the creases of the parched land, looking up; from between rivets of rain, wiping our eyes.

12. With humility.

13. And with hope. Oh, yes, always with hope.

Brooklyn girls

Those Brooklyn girls are greedy, they get
their sights set on Manhattan, don't let
a little thing like a river get in their way. They
marshal all over, Coney Island, Canarsie,
Flatbush and Bed Stuy, roll down Eastern Parkway
and through the Grand Army Plaza a triumphant
tribe, gather on the Heights and plunge right in,
lemmings. They can walk on water, those girls,
they turn their size 4s into skis and glide across,
pelicans skating on shiny fish, come wringing
their teased hair out on Bowling Green, straighten
their pantyhose and head north, toward where
some visionary has erected tall buildings, markers.
They know what they want and how to get it, just
ask the Brooklyn boys they leave behind. Their eyes
are coal mines but they can see forever.

The swimmers

Two teenage girls in swimsuits their mothers
couldn't object to stand at the water's edge, splashing
each other innocently while their bodies call out
to the passersby, *look at me, look at me.* What is
to be done? To look or to look away, to follow
the impulse of biology or the whisper in the ear
of civility, of civilization? Their laughter floats
on the summer air.

Bait

The owl takes the bait and is as suddenly
in the biologist's hands as the mouse had been
in the owl's beak. Stunned, the hunter,
now the hunted, quivers in the cage
of fingers, faces and voices pressing down
on it, the thrill of fear piercing its heart.
The rumble rising in its throat fools
no one, its talons pinned in strong hands
beyond beak's reach, it's as powerless
as any prey of its own and it knows it,
is resigned to the moment of its death,
the tearing apart it would not hesitate
to do. When that doesn't happen, when
suddenly the grip dissolves and the owl
explodes into the air, that is the moment
religion enters its narrow world, when
it's seduced into belief.

Addressee unknown

When the annual Christmas card comes
from the Williams you'll no longer be receiving
mail and the envelope will go back to them
marked "addressee unknown" like a boomerang
oiled with surprise. You can imagine the expression
on their faces, good old Fred and doughty Doris,
your neighbours in the first drafty apartment
in Strathcona, your tablemates on the cruise
up the inner passage. How Doris laughed
at your lame jokes, making you wonder
if you'd made the wrong choice, and how Fred,
not to be undone, made a fool of himself trying
to flirt. All those years of cards, the promises
of visits thankfully not fulfilled,
the transmogrification of children captured
through their ages in photos, caterpillar
to butterfly, butterfly to caterpillar.
And now this, a returned card, all the good will
of the year zippered into one succinct greeting
and even that not enough, not enough to find its way
through the constructed maze from their house
to yours, all the obstacles you've set up, the false
starts and endings, addressee unknown, unknowable.

Moscow was burning

The old men moved slowly from the darkness
of the marsh, muffled in the heavy clothing
of night, their teeth like the submerged roots
of the stout willows behind them, to tell us
Moscow was burning, that it was finally safe
to go home. That evening we lay on our backs
in tall grass and watched the stars pit the face
of the sky, Adams without Edens, without
grace, dreaming of the men we had once
been, the women we had longed for, children
we could never be. In our hands, the ache
of emptiness, our eyes full with the blank stare
back of the mirror, our shoulders rejoicing
at the lifting of weight. There is a beauty
in that night, a certain beauty we've been told of
but never see, a guitar song of nightingales
hidden in the folds of their own throats. We lay
in that damp grass long past the whimpering
in our bones, long past the siren whisper
of sleep, long past the nightingale's final flight
of fancy, leading us back the way we had come.

The contender

Think of Brando in *Waterfront* or *Streetcar*,
the delicate curl of his lip, then in *The Freshman*,
bloated, stale. A life in a nutshell, a caution
against growing old. Monroe had the better idea,
live fast, go out quick, leave a beautiful idea.
Bogey coughing out his lungs, Bob Hope
squeezed as a lemon, Ronnie Reagan a child
in arms again, where's the romance in that?
The wisdom? Brando fled to the South Seas
but kept coming back, found he couldn't flee
himself. *Stella*, he cried, *Stella*, but there was
no reply, Stella herself having gone gracefully
into the curtains where he couldn't follow.
On his deathbed, he dreamt of Wally Cox,
whose ashes awaited his.

The singing
(with apologies to David Carpenter)

In the snow where there had hitherto
only been white, today, a speck of red
that inflames Yacov's imagination. Without
thought or hesitation he stoops to retrieve it
though should the guard see him it could mean
death, a quick rifle-butt to the head
at the very least. In the palm of his hand
the strange object glows, pulses, sings to him
until he is able to deftly insert it in a tear
in his collar where he has fashioned a pocket
for scraps of food, and from its resting place
on his neck it sings to him all day. Later,
in his bunk, he can examine the talisman
at his leisure, a cigarette butt, no more than
4 centimetres long, one end blackened
into crumbling ash that comes away
as soot on his fingertip at his lightest touch
but the other end—and this is the wonder,
the magic, the miracle—a smear of lipstick
still ripe with the smell of the woman who
wore it when Yacov brings the marvel
to his nostrils, still moist from her lips
and oh how the thought of those lips
thrills him. In the morning, in deep snow
again, the work gang trudging to the mine,
he allows himself a quick forbidden glance
at the sky and postulates this theory: a jet
filled with beautiful people from Milan
and Venice pursuing the sunrise across
the Siberian sky, the woman a Venetian
with dark tumbling hair, breasts
and wasp-waist sculpted from snow,

the pungent cigarette taking on new fragrance
as it soaked in the urine of the beautiful woman
who flushed into the frigid crystal air, the urine
falling as heavenly ice across the dark forest,
the cigarette butt with its lipstick testament
falling with the unerring aim of angels
into the path of Yacov, six years
into a ten-year sentence for petty theft
and innumerable other sins only he knows
about. As he works today and tomorrow
and for days later he savours the thought
of what this new currency might bring
him, pictures the delight and wonder in the eyes
of Chernofsky and Schmuel and the others
as they bring the blood-red smear of musk
and oil and sex to their noses, sniffing delicately,
hefting the precious relic in their palms,
weighing the possibilities. Possibility! And
from across the endless expanse
of frozen snow, from deep within
the blackest bowels of the mine, from
its safe nest in his collar, Yacov can hear
the singing.

Screenplay by King

The dream—*the nightmare!*—unfolds
like a Stephen King movie, quietly, building
suspense, with its own logic. There are
small creatures, horrible, the product
of special effects, and once they attach
themselves they drain the life from you
and can't be detached, become
your Siamese twin. What wakes you
is the sound of screaming, not your own
but one of the characters, a young woman
attacked in her tub. The creature is no bigger
than a leech at first, but grows quickly,
the size of a kitten, a child, and then
the woman appears to be embracing
a younger version of the actress playing
her role, then making love with a mirror,
and all the while she is screaming
to be separated from herself. When you
do finally awake you shake your head
with the usual disbelief, it was so real,
you could see every detail, it really *was*
like a movie, the characters and storyline
all unknown to you, based on a novel
you've never read. You're shaken, have
a glass of water and sit on the edge of the bed
trying to think of something else, anything
to get the last wisps of dream out of your head,
not the screaming so much as the certainty
that you too are permanently attached
to yourself.

Homecoming

So she came home. The old people greeted
her as if nothing had happened, as if no time
at all had passed, and it was possible for her
to imagine nothing had, that life had been
just a dream from which she had now awoken.
There were calls and letters but she didn't answer,
tore them up unread, and as the sun rose and fell
in its peculiar rhythm the dream began to fade,
a photograph left too long in the sun. Finally,
she was allowed to close her eyes again and see
only stars.

Six degrees of separation

Wascana Creek where it passes by my window
is no wider than the thickness of my finger, no more
of a threat, a body of water that is more a thought
of a body than any physical dimension you could feel,
a creek so small a man with an ox and cart seeking
a ford might well be three miles past before he realizes
he'd come to it, passed over, been transformed
and barely got the wheels of his wagon wet, a creek
always last to be called, last to be chosen for basketball
or anything else, thinner than any hope you ever
thought you had. Buffalo stopped in their meditations
here to drink but were immediately afterwards thirsty
again, and their droppings fell like clots of chalk, coyotes
paused by these banks to consider the oblique mysteries
of life, to compose maddening riddles with pens dipped
in its invisible ink, dusty Cree and Assiniboine dismounted
to laugh at the joke they were leaving white-eyes
in their wake. This is a creek as far from an ocean
as it is from the moon, with the difference that the moon
shines above it, that it lifts its watery breast to the caresses
of the moon, that it hides its moist face
from the moon's smirking gaze, while the oceans
are beyond sight, sound, smell, even the ghost
of an ocean is beyond the reach of this creek.

Except that this isn't so. The Wascana crawls its way
across the prairie and falls exhausted into the open arms
of the Qu'Appelle, not much bigger but imbued
with more purpose, that purpose being to pour its own heart
out onto the shoulder of the South Saskatchewan which
rises at Prince Albert into the bed of its Northern lover,
and from there, like a spit of sperm battling its way
to the womb the Wascana embodied in all that water
travels as a prince, a knight templar on crusade
to the holy land all the way to the throat-clearing roar
of the Churchill, cascading into the icy heart of
Hudson Bay and the Arctic, just a stone's throw beyond.
This is a creek then with ancestral knowledge stamped
into its DNA. It is humble and knows it, but knows too
that it is part of something larger. At night, when the
stars come out to drink, the creek fills itself up
with their light, basking in reflected glory. It dreams
of its journey, its stagnant heart frothing against stone.
It dreams of destination, the welcome arms of its mother.

Smoking

Smoking in the girls' room
Sandie has a science lesson
better than any Mr. McArthur
ever performed in the steaming lab
with hissing Bunsen burners
under beakers of air expanding
and contracting like the lungs
of the girls now, sucking smoke in,
blossoming it out, but that's not it.
All the goldfish bowls are filled
with exotic brine and fish, "gross"
way too mild a word for it, but Sandie
and her friends have to go, that's
all there is to it, the problem
in a nutshell, as Mr. McArthur likes
to say. Janice holds her nose,
fills her hand with toilet paper
and flushes, "evening the playing
field," she quips, slathers the seat
with paper and perches above. Tammy
finds the best of the bad lot, shrugs,
holds her nose and crouches. But Sandie
takes the path of least resistance, recalling
Mr. McArthur's adage that the solution
that seems the simplest is often the best,
slipping down her jeans and hoisting herself
up to the cold steel sink, turns on both taps
and lets the liquids within and without
co-mingle, just the way they would
in a more ordered world.

                    The girls wash
up, flick their butts into the torrent
and soberly weigh the evidence
of their experiment, evidence that seems
to suggest they can be the doers
rather than the done. Still, the question
of the fish themselves remain. "Always
look beyond the obvious," McArthur
likes to say, and that's what keeps ringing
in Sandie's head through the rest of the day,
keeps her up deep into the night, the fish,
the fish, the fish. When she wakes,
an answer tentative as the dawn seems
to have formed in the back of Sandie's mind,
an answer slippery as the fish themselves.

Oedipus

Harsh evening and through famished dust
I see the brightening eyes of birds
too far away to identify. What attracts
them is my swollen foot, the bloodied socket
of my eye, the broken saxophone
of my mouth where my call to them
lingers, still working itself into code neither I
nor they can decipher. When the teeth
and tongue get the sense of it, those birds
will know all they need.

Doing better

The regretted remark, the hairy eyeball
meant for someone else, the unexpected fall
against the shoulder once too often. We come
home from life bruised, replaying the tape.
Under the covers, the radiators popping,
we wonder if we couldn't have been
better, know it's true, make resolutions
the wake-up radio scares away. Still, we
try, go forth to the world without armor,
just our best intentions.

West by west

Oh give me a home, a rope, a drink
of water from the cold well, a biscuit
with gravy and coffee in a tin cup too hot
to hold. The stars blazing spears, the moon
a surprised O in the darkened sky's mouth.
A coyote telegraphing its grief
for the disappearing bison, the teeth
of barbed wire, rust blooming on tin cans
in the dump where the bears gorge themselves
like teenagers at the drive-in. This is
West, the sun sets here, tipping its hat, its eye
cerise from lack of sleep, puffy with contempt.
West, where young men quake, where the rest
of the dream still shows its colour, West,
where Prairies shoulder themselves into hills
and mountains, wash down to the overbearing sea
that holds all our attention finally, pulling
the night around its tender bare neck. West,
where whatever is pursuing gives up
the chase.

At Frost's grave, Bennington, Vermont

He had a lover's quarrel with the world.
You have to squint to make out the letters
cut in stone above Frost's grave, the inscription
suggesting the great man went to his death
still nursing a grudge. There are dates, his own,
and, around the large stone, smaller ones
for wife and children, one who died young.
Frost rests, if rest is what it is, on a slight incline
in a grassy field filled with such stone, a rich crop.
Some date back to the Revolution, and there are
many from the Civil War and later conflicts, and here
is this poet whose only argument was with his lover.
The church is old, plain, proud of its plainness,
perhaps a bit ashamed of its pride, one of the sins
warned against. The grass has that recently cut
smell of deep June, and mosquitoes and flies
are bivouacked under the trees, chattering
the air, the sky impossibly blue and cloudless.
Except for the company you would keep
it might be irresistible to lie down here
and consider that empty sky, consider a quarrel
you know you cannot win. A *lover's quarrel*
he had, and here he lies, while the world spins on.

The elements

Rough weather

The rain is a whore, slanting
her blue-green eyes, drumming
her fingers along the swell
of her lacy breast.

The wind is a whore, lifting
her skirt, a flash of thigh
and billows of eggwhite
in your eye.

Snow is a whore, the frost
of her teeth bitter as she
smiles, a smear of lipstick
on the incisor.

August sun is a whore, her ringed hand
splayed across your back, the nail
of each finger carving
her initials.

Into this rough weather
I throw myself, breathless,
expectant.

Lucky old sun

In the field and meadow the sun takes
giant steps, he strides with his chest
stuck out, arms swinging. Over the ocean
and rivers, he rolls like a retriever puppy
on his back, the sun, his pink tongue out
with happiness. Above the mountains
and hills and in the furred valleys he rides
his bicycle, no hands, doing headstands
on the saddle. In the desert, the sun
practices ballet, one fearless *pointe*
after another, a *pas de deux* with himself.

But in the forest the sun is timid, slinking
from tree to tree, his fingers trembling,
white as a ghost.

Seventy is nothing
       (for Pat Krause)

Seventy is nothing really—consider Methuselah,
the great white whale, the disillusioned stars
in their bored circuits. But seventy is a great deal more
than the span of a cat, the expectation of the aphid,
if it has any, a great deal more than where you ever
thought you might be. Seventy is relative, then, more
than this, less than that, but what consolation
is there in that? It's not seventy that matters
anyway, but the day after, the day after seventy,
and the day after that. Yes, the day after that.

Extremes

Breakfast at 7, lunch at noon, the day
measures itself out as Eliot said
in teaspoons, teaspoons and tablespoons,
grapefruit rinds and coffee grounds
and crusts of bread, the long hopeful day
unraveling into night and the prospect
of it all beginning again. You go
to the mirror and see not yourself
but some semblance, a wisp, a reminder
of the person you were, the person
who went to extremes. *Extreme* now
is only a measuring spoon, the white-hot ends
of a clear glass tube within which moderation
fills an ever-expanding middle, mercury
languishing in a temperate zone, not
too cold, not too hot.
Not too hot, just hot enough.
Perfect.

The four elements

In the morning, the child saw the world
for what it was: sky and land and water
but she didn't see fire, couldn't hear or feel
it, had no sense of it at all. She played
in the meadow with a ball, she and her friend
skipped rope, the dog did tricks for them
and there were sandwiches under the trees
and cool lemonade. A boat ride, a trip
to the zoo, an errand to the store, cold chicken
and biscuits for supper, a story before bed.
Only then, as she curled in the twilight before
sleep did she hear the turning of the wheels,
feel the heat.

Bad luck dog
(after Dianne Warren)

The bad luck that followed you
like a stray dog from the edge of town
moved into the house, sat on its haunches
in the kitchen as you ate your toast
and tea, watching with a sadness you
couldn't have known about, licking
its chops. The thing of it is
that you love dogs, are always taking
in runaways and castoffs, nursing
back to health that beagle crushed
by a hit and run last summer, there's
nothing you like more than to get down
on the floor and smell the sweet milk breath
of a puppy, its belly soft and exposed
as yours was to the jaws of this black mutt
with its warts and mange, its indifferent bark,
its faraway gaze.

Saskatchewan weather report

A day so hot
the goldfish bubbled
in the bowl and offered
up fish and chips.

A night so cold
the curve of the moon
froze to the tip
of the wind's tongue.

A wind so high
the trees tore out
their roots and offered
them up to the sky.

Dust so black
you could die of thirst
just opening
a window.

A sky so clear
the sun shone till Sunday
and back again
before closing its eyes.

A day so fine
the afternoon dug in
its heels, refused
to follow the morning.

A love so rare
even June
blushed
at the thought.

Hollow bones
     (for Mary Drover)

A bud of pain blossoms in your bones
like a snatch of song nagging your mind
for recognition, refusing to go away.
In your flesh there is a promise of comfort,
the wing of a bird bathing itself in dust
to balm this insistent heat. The bones
of the bird are hollow, free of pain
or comfort, free of the will to explode
or implode, free of everything but absence
and the need to fill itself, to sprout feather
and wing and the joyous song
of morning, a song you catch yourself,
later, whistling.

Hands, mouth, teeth

The small hands of the rain
tap on the window, tap
through the blind night
then pound till blood
seeps from the knuckles,
the glass hardening
its transparent heart.

The small mouth of the wind
whispers at the door, calls
your name so that you start,
the vision of the ghost
dancing on your grave
as clear as a wish, a wish
unfulfilled.

The small teeth of the animal
growing within you chatter
with fright, with delight, with
rumination, with hunger. They
bare themselves to your tongue,
but shyly, an awkward girl
at her first dance.

Making dirt
(for Betsy Rosenwald)

The world is filled with dirt but not all dirt
works the way dirt should, that's the way
the set designer explains it—it tends to blow
away, for one thing, and turn to mud, you can
see that, so here you are, your arms already
aching from days of painting, 12-hour days
with a crew that doesn't always get it, and
you're a kid again, playing in the dirt, but it's
a dirt of your own devising, a quart each
of water and Wellbond, a pint of fine Rolatex
and a scoop of medium, a five-pound bag
of plaster of Paris, as much raw umber colorant
as it takes, a bit of paper maché and a dollop
of joint compound, stirred well in a tub, down
on your knees painting this goop into the set,
a roped off square the actors playing archaeologists
will be digging in when the action begins, dirt
without character or history but weight, definite
weight. It's hard then not to think about the nature
of dirt, the deserted farmhouse you pass on the edge
of town, its grey boards crumbling under their
own weight and the implacable tide of weather,
the impermanence of all flesh, your own
included, the flakes of dead skin snowdrifting
from your scalp, hairs, microscopic droplets
of oil and mucous, this shower of detritus
trailing behind you like a shadow, the forces
of decay arrayed against you, the double vision
that plagues you some nights, the ache in your
knee and the deeper aches you don't want
to think about at all, your own body crumbling
as surely, as mercilessly, as barnboards, the paint
stripped right off your skin, dust to dust, the passing
of all things, even dirt made on command.

80

Mushrooms

Rain and more rain, then an explosion
of mushrooms, yellow, orange, brown,
curls of flesh a gnome's ear, skin
translucent, mocking the sun,
the lovelier the more deadly.
In this green kingdom of the forest,
the mushroom is king, not the tree,
ruling from below not above.
Flora and fauna, even cougar
and bear beat a wide circle
around the mushroom, giving it
respect, its reach so much more
than mere tongue and gut can
comprehend. Only rain speaks
the mushroom's language, whispering
lies and blandishments, inducements.
The Bible got so much wrong, in the garden
it was the mushroom forbidden, not
the apple; original sin, imagination.

Floating in land
(for Robin Poitras)

They put chains around your legs
but you slipped free and danced.
They tied you to poles, put lead weights
around your shoulders but you shrugged
and wriggled, and you danced. They nailed
your feet to the smooth boards of the stage
but you smiled through the pain, left
footprints like lipstick kisses where you
deigned to touch down, falling back
into yourself. Chains again—they
wrapped you in them, padlocks, then
like Houdini, into a safe, the combination
thrown away, the safe lifted by a crane
into a tank of water where fish of the most
brilliant colours swam, as if to taunt you. But
again you made the impossible look easy.
In the water, you grew gills and fins,
as in the air you would affect the use
of wings. Floating in land, you
transformed it into water, into air,
into fire.

Sister moon

The moon consumes the best of itself, leaves
the rest alone, slinks away into the night
licking its wounds. The sun's another matter.
It gobbles the sky, the better part of the day gone
before that ball of fire has even stretched
its arms. It rolls across the hills and plateaus
as if it had all the time in the world, pausing
to smell the lilies of one valley, stirring up
a wind in another, licks its lips, yawns, comes
back with a second appetite, belching
politely. The sun fills up the day, exhausts
the day, cuts the day off at the knees. Next
to the sun, the moon is a lady.

Being

I don't do, Brenda says her brother says,
*I just am. Some people are doers, some
are be-ers. That's enough for me.* He's
a dry drunk, failed farmer, 40s, lives
with his mother, satisfied or, if not satisfied,
content. Nice enough fellow but not much going
on is an understatement. It takes two days
for the words to sink in. I'm on the beach
gazing at the lake, waiting for the top in my mind
to stop spinning, waiting to be still. I want,
it comes to me, to just *be.* I think of zen,
of being part of the water, of the trees,
of the horizon, to be one with all around
me, but that isn't it, I realize, this is
something deeper, or shallower, something
else, being one merely with yourself. Thinking
about it undermines it, it is *doing,* thinking,
just *being* is something more, or less,
something else, something the daffodil
has mastered, something the willow does
without effort, something the owl knows
the answer to when he cries *who, who.*

84

Black ice

The city is running with ice today, whatever restraint
you may have felt yesterday gone, the car a skater
wild on a pond, the possibilities of the intersection
endless. Your heart is in your throat but the brakes
are nowhere to be found, a promise unfulfilled,
and stopping without harm only a hope. All of this
academic, though, on the deserted street at this
ungodly hour, dawn not yet fully in motion,
the skating rink all your own and the admiring cheers
of the judges for you alone, the reckless wind
raising your blood for a fierce abandoned moment
until the dog darts across your line of sight, the veer
and the bootless slide begins and in peripheral vision
there is the first unformed image of the child, the end
of the leash in her hand.

White on white

In town, the snow begins to grey
almost the moment it sets down, as if
forbidden from too much seductiveness.
Out here, it holds its whiteness deep
into February and March, the fields
frosted with cream you might gladly
drown in. The whiteness an idea of itself
colourless water is just beginning
to dream, an idea crystallizing
into shape one side at a time until
there are six sides to the argument
it cannot win and it puffs itself
up with pride, false pride
because all it did really was slow
down, allowing the coldness within
itself to emerge. Why white, so
white? So white the eye rebels
against absorbing it all, white
as sheets, as bandages before the splash
of blood, white as the breasts
of partridges, as love before
the kiss, white as heat that bows
its head.

The tick

I heard the meadowlark sing
this morning, the distant drone
of the highway white noise evaporating
into the fulsome air. Where a skunk
had passed a perfume rich as lavender
still hung, uncertain of its direction
and intent. On the russet body of a doe
lifting its shy head to sniff the masked air
a tick burrowed deep into fur, nothing
uncertain as to its purpose. It neither
considered its choices nor hesitated
out of pity, neither listened nor sniffed
the quivering air but drove on, blind
as armies, as ruthless. I turned away, walked
on, ignorant of the deception.

Aurora borealis

Morning's milky blue belies the blazing sky
of midnight, the canvas washed clean of moon,
stars, a pulsing light from the north. Opening
our crusted eyes, it's this truth we face,
not the remembered other, the painful throb
of imagination. In the distant night,
we were children exclaiming passionate
but empty abstractions, heard words
like *truth* and *beauty* escaping our parched lips,
danced like innocents in the pale summer darkness.
The harsh light of morning asks more of us, asks
us to make sense not only of what we saw but
what we *didn't* see, the glimmer of angry light behind
the vibrato of aurora borealis, the hungry lips
of the hunter moon lurking within
the harvest moon's benign smile, the smile
of the pretty girl dancing in the grass, her feet
just barely touching the ground.

Tea and sympathy

Herb tea, luke-warm sympathy
and the whole wide world watching
via internet, things really aren't
what they used to be. Even millennia
have lost their punch, no riots
in the streets, no mass hysteria
or rash of stigmata. The universe
unfolds not so much as it should
but as the boys at the Berkeley lab
say it will, their eyes glued
to the stars for revelations measured
out in decimals and fractions,
not coffee spoons, the Big Bang
continuing to flex its muscles
through an eternity only it
can imagine, elbow room
at last.

The hunger

So cold your face stings, your gloved hands
numb in the heartless sun and you wonder
how the chickadees can open their mouths
to sing without freezing their throats, and what
do they have to sing about anyway
or are those cries of pain as they crowd
the blanketed branches of the firs
along the road where you walk? Pain
or joy, or the constant humming thrum
of assertion against the cold, wings
against the aching blue of sky, the opening
void, the hunger.

The vanity of trees

In the frigid night, the invisible forces
of weather shifted gears and the air wept.
By first light the trees had turned
to porcelain, the quiet city now noisy
with white-bearded old men standing
at lazy attention, rattling their canes
and calling out their names,
Howard and *Thomas* and *Robert*
and *John, John, John.* In the din
it was easy to forget they were only trees,
really, playing a part, thrusting out
their hoary chests, convincing themselves
it was spring and they were young men
again, resplendent in their coats
of green, so vain. Then the sun rose
and they trembled.

The hour

This is the hour not of death, no,
that we pray is years away, and not
even of its premonition, that too years
away, in the past, but of its opposite,
the hour of life unyielding, the day
stretching ahead to an unimagined horizon
beyond which there is still more ripple
of this unflagging muscle. The phone
at last lies mute in its cradle, the open letter
innocent on the table. In the distance
a bird calls, one ambiguous note
that is certainly not of alarm or fear,
that could as easily be of joy as of mourning,
of hunger as of complaint, and it is that song
which fills this hour, forcing you to listen.

Morning in the Retreat House

Morning in the Retreat House arrives with a clarity
any other dwelling might envy. The curtains
over the east windows become wings
and the walls give way to the insistence
of sun, liquefying, the skin of morning burning
from your eyes. The bed upon which you
have slept turns translucent, becomes a cloud,
a meadow of clover, a current of water floating
you into yourself. The furnace hums but there is
no warmth, only scented breeze, the distant song
of birds at their labour, a heat of joy. Light
pulses, an aurora borealis of sun. If there is magic
in the world, this is when it transpires, the window
a projector, the wall above the bed a screen,
the whole panoply of possibility playing
and you becoming yourself at last.

Where the heart goes

The romance of sport

My love is the moment before
the pitch, that instant
of perfect stillness
when the pitcher
weighs the balances, decides,
nods—

your love is the snap.

Shoulda, woulda, coulda

Shoulda loved you better, woulda
if I coulda, but I couldn't
and there it is, did my best
and what more could I do? You
coulda loved me better, you
shoulda, but you didn't and there
it is, you did what you could
and what more could you do? We
coulda loved each other better,
shoulda, but we didn't, woulda
if we coulda but we couldn't, didn't
and there it is, did the best we could
and what more could we do? Don't
look at me that way.

Where the heart goes

To the corner, a penciled list crushed
in its hand, a hopeful look playing
about its lips. To the greengrocer,
the butcher's, the heavenly bakery
where a head can ache with the smell
of so much goodness. To the chiropodist,
the chiropractor, the Church of Jesus Christ,
Scientist, where you imagine an ascetic man
with an anemic beard and a white coat,
a skeptical expression, Glenn Gould hands.
To the rocky south of France
in winter, all the poor pores of your body
ready to burst with gratitude, the muscles
around your mouth stretched into a permanent
smile. To the cash machine, the off-sale, to hell
and back on a fast freight, to the ends
of the earth, to the corner, where
it waits and waits.

A winter of discontent

Snow confettis the crystal air, it fills
the open arms of the sidewalk, powders
the blue hair of the dowager tree, sugars
the channels and grooves of the car, fisting
the lock shut. There is no way to keep up
with it, shovel and broom shy in its presence,
just as the windows rattle beneath the scrape
of the wind's finger along the aching glass
and the molten heart of the furnace bursts
with fear of the cold always licking, licking
at the house's chapped skin.

But this is a winter of discontent that goes
far beyond the elements, cuts right through
any contrived defence, settles its cold breath
deep in the flesh and bone. You wake
on your side of the bed, I on mine, two beds
as far apart as if they were on the two sides
of a shivering moon. The phone is our link
and when it rings I hear the shattering
of ice, the slow pulse of blood beneath
it. There are only so many ways to say
I love you, but each one of them is true,
each one a small flame cupped in my hand.

The way love is

A balming breeze on feverish skin,
cold wind razoring your face,
that's the way love is. Soft fingers,
a fist. The way you turned to me
in the night, the turning
away. Your name a whisper,
a cry, a shout, a prayer,
a promise.

Lilacs don't bloom here

Lilacs don't bloom here in April.
That fragrant spring we remember
is from another place, another time,
another life. The iridescent throat
of the hummingbird, the red breast
of the robin, even the purple velvet
of the crocus, they are not for us
this year, an April without colour
or scent. Oh, yes, our spring lives,
but in memory, where the aroma
of lilac has not faded, the heat
of that day we cherish rises still
into a cerulean sky finger-painted
with watery cloud. A white dress,
a borrowed ring, a broken branch
of lilac, a glass of beer reddened
with tomato juice and all that we
could muster of our selves, you
and I forever in some amber eye
of memory, the heavenly perfume
of lilacs transporting us to a heaven
of our own design, our own choosing.

Head over heels

This is off the top of my head
the way the light ignites the air,
the way the dust rebels, choking
the broom, the way the river runs
upstream, daring its banks to foreclose.

This is off the top of my head
the way history spins down
to this very moment, the way you show
your teeth when you smile, the way
the moon hides its head in shame.

This is off the top of my head
the way the moon turns itself on
and off, the way the stars squint
into the passing lane, the sun
heaving its melodramatic sighs.

This is off the top of my head
the way you nod *your* head, shake
your head, bow your head, the way
the light radiates around your head
as if forming a halo for the world,
spreading its arms to the world,
the way you tilt your head just so.

Heart's warning

The heart in its nest, the sun
an egg in a blue bowl, the world
according to plan, the bone free
in its velvet socket. Then a sudden
narrowing of the eyes. There is design
in the madness it takes a lifetime
to ken, purpose to the tooth
but still the teeth tear at our flesh,
still we fall. The heart in its nest
calls out a warning, love is
the listening,
the rising.

Eyes full of birds

The sky is raining sparrows, a storm
of them around our feeder, a blizzard
of brown and grey feathers, the rustle
of their feet on the tin, the crackle
of their feeding, their song. My heart
is breaking—oh, never mind
why—but my eyes are full
of birds.

Beautiful

You have always been the girl you
never wanted to be. Too short, too fat,
too dark for belief. Too tall, too thin, so
fair you couldn't go out in the sun
without melting. You never knew enough,
couldn't laugh because of your teeth. You
loved to dance but the only ones who asked
were the wrong ones, so ungainly. There was
never enough, never the right thing, never
any thing real. Nothing fit. You always said
the wrong thing or nothing at all. You
stayed home and wished you were there,
went there and wished you were home.
Life stretched out like the languid body
of a doe in the road, the blood congealed
on her mouth, but you shook that thought
off, went on. You have never been the girl
you wanted to be, but there is a light
when you turn a certain way, and you are,
you know, so beautiful,
so beautiful.

Music of water

If my mind were as clear as the water
in this stream, if my thoughts were as clear,
my intentions, my words, you would not
hesitate, dear, but take my hand, secure
in the knowledge my intentions were
pure, pure as the water in this stream,
as the light in your eye, as my light. Purity
and clarity, clarity and purity,
and the music of water over stones.

What I miss

The way the sun slants across your name
as I hold it in my mouth, the taste
of you in my eyes, my ears, the sound
of your breathing in my chest
as I run, the hiss and hum, the fullness of you
in my bath, in the wrinkles of the bed
as I comb it out in the morning, the texture
of you in the coffee cup as the cream ribbons
through it, the rhythm of you as it lingers
on the pillow, in your shadow
on the grass, on the snow, the mystery
of you, the riddle, the answer.

Vanity

A woman half his age
on his arm, the painter juts
his chin at the sun, taking
its measure one squint
at a time. This is his time
now, skill, fame and age
all coming together finally
in a design as pleasing as any
he might make himself, something
to remember. In the locker room
mirror he frowns at the grey hairs
on his chest but the chest itself
is powerful and in the pool
where he marvels at her suppleness
he swims like a porpoise beside
her, his arms as strong as ever, and he
sees his reflection in her eyes. This
is the life not as he dreamed it
might be—that was the scuffling,
the egg sandwiches and vino,
the closed-for-lunch sign
on the gallery door—but as he
feared, so much finally
to lose.

A promise

Love isn't a promise, love is,
life isn't a promise, it just is
and she prayed to understand this
—Wendy McNeil, "She prayed"

But it is, love *is* a promise, a promise
you keep breaking, that you forget
and remember and forget. Best intentions
are all the heart is wrapped in, naked
beneath the gift-wrap, the gaudy bow. And life,
life is a promise too, the clutch of air
in the lungs, the rising of blood, the way
the eyes swoon at the sight of whatever
we secretly desire, every sensation
conjoining to deceive us into believing
it will go on forever, then softly closing
the door. These are promises to build
a life on, promises to get us past
the shudder each day brings, the glimpse
of the shadow, promises we can hold
each other to, even when we fail
to deliver. *I love you*, that trite thought
no idle promise, no promise going
for broke, no boast, not a prayer
but an answer.

Land mines

Long after she left, the mines
she'd planted began to explode
in his face, the inscription
on the flyleaf of a book she'd bought
for his birthday, *with love, always,*
in her unmistakable hand, her initials
inside a heart etched on the inside
of his watchband, warmed by the pulse
in his wrist, the saltcellar in the shape
of a rooster she'd bought that time
in Saskatchewan, the pepper long
gone too, he and that disconsolate cock
gazing at each other over the empty
plate. The closets were bare of her clothes
but filled with a scent he knew so well,
apple blossoms. One silver crescent moon
still dangling in the dust beneath the sofa;
in the bathroom a twisted tube of toothpaste,
her brand, all but empty, hard as cement
now. But these were just the pieces of her
he could see and touch, what about the song
forever on the radio they'd danced to
that night at the boss's party, what about
the genuine scent of apple blossoms
on the spring air, the chant of waves
on rocks? She was everywhere
and he was nowhere, his foot
suspended in air

Home and garden

The bear in her cave, licking her honey lips,
the wolf in her den, sharpening her teeth,
the cunning fox in her lair, dreaming of leading
hounds a merry chase, the bird in her nest,
orchestrating her song. And you, on your feet,
at home in your house of shining bones,
in your skin, crossing the street,
rearranging the furniture.

To the station

To the station and back is half an hour
but the train can be counted on
to be late so she always brings the paper
or a detective novel to fill the time
as she waits, that and the company
of the radio, news and the drive-home music
and chatter drawing her in, even,
on what she expects to be the worst nights,
the rack of knitting that never ends,
raveling and unraveling over and over,
a sleeve that will never fit, always too long
or too short, anything to avoid the thought
of what he might have to say.

Wreckless moon

See that moon up there, that sly
half-ass of a moon, that sonuvabitch
of a moon with seeds in its teeth, that
damn-fool of a moon-eyed moon, pie-eyed
moon, piss-faced moon, that shit-eating grin
of a moon, tight-lipped moon, tight-assed moon,
uptight moon, damn straight hullaballoo
of a moon, oh, she's a bugger of a moon,
a ball-buster, a heart-breaker, a heartless moon,
a reckless moon, a goddamn train wreck of a moon
oh, she's a bitch, that moon, cold-hearted,
bloody-minded witch of a moon, slut,
that's what she is, that moon, shining
for anybody who'll look up. Damn
that moon, goddamn that moon, damn
her pretty eyes.

Scars

(a found poem–for Mark & Elona)

We take it day by day. Most days
I think we're healing. But there are
scars for both of us. Always there are
scars.
    And on the scars
of broken trees, moss grows.

A boy in Danville*

A boy in Danville broke her heart
but she carried on like it was nothing,
as if it didn't mean a thing. She set
her lips, went to the business college
and found a good job with a lawyer,
took in a boarder. There was still Mom
to look after, sick and alone, and Bobby
and John to see through school but
you never heard her complain. Years
passed and the nieces and nephews
were as good as her own. Mom died
and she took in another boarder, folks
talked about her pies. The lawyer
went to Florida and she sat on the porch
in the rocker a nephew brought her,
reading a novel, thinking about Danville,
the music, the flying feet.

*"A boy in Danville broke her heart" was sparked by "A boy in
Danville broke my heart," a line in the poem "Square Dancing
in Naperville" from Keeping in Touch by Eugene McNamara.

Taking chances

I take my chances, take a chance
on you taking a chance on me, take
a chance I can be what you hope
I'll be, the chance I can be more
than I am. I cut the deck, rattle
my lucky dice, throw the whole saltcellar
of luck to the winds of chance, let
myself fall into their embrace,
let my chips fall, where they may,
where they must not.

Spring in the seasons of trees

The mouths of the cottonwoods explode
into deserts, speechless cliffs of chalk,
their throats canyons of salt. Their hearts
wither, turn to dust underfoot. I am the seed
you spit from your acid tongue, the aftertaste
you can't get rid of, the bitter smell. I am
the speck of grit in your eye, that irritation.
And you, you are the new leaf, so tender,
so green.

What moves

What moves through you like a dancer
walks through me, heavy-footed. What moves
through me like a gambler shuffling his deck
moves through you like a magician, quicker
than the eye. You are quick to my silver,
me base metal, you alchemy, I am
chemistry, you magic. To your hare
I can be a snare, I know, a lion
to your gazelle, and I will myself to go
slower, to move through you like a wind
rustling softly in the aspen leaves, to allow
your deft movement through me.

Until we shine

It's only a matter of time until we shine.
—*"Shine," Tom Wilson & Colin Cripps*
(Junkhouse)

The heavens conspire against us, thickening
their tongues. Our eyes too thicken, darken
with cloud, clouding our minds, forcing
the pierced lightning we pin our hopes on
to streak ahead, out of reach. Our necks numb
from looking up, looking out, our eyes
sore from disuse, still the brilliance promised
eludes us, too shy for scrutiny. And yet
the promise rings, clapper in a bell
of brass and gold hiccuping its discordant chime
across the stuttered snow, urging us on
to whatever doom or ecstasy lies around
the next turn and the next. Until we
are blind, and even then the phantom
glow entices us, memory of a light
not yet seen. Shine, yes, even with all light
extinguished, we would.

120